MOUNT RAINIER NATIONAL PARK
ACTIVITY BOOK

PUZZLES, MAZES, GAMES, AND MORE ABOUT MOUNT RAINIER NATIONAL PARK

NATIONAL PARKS ACTIVITIES SERIES

MOUNT RAINIER NATIONAL PARK ACTIVITY BOOK

LITTLE BISON
Press

For more free national parks activities, visit
www.littlebisonpress.com

About Mount Rainier National Park

Mount Rainier National Park is located in the state of Washington. The park's namesake mountain is an active volcano and stretches 14,410 feet into the sky. The mountain goes by many names, including Tahoma, Tacoma, and Tacobet.

Mount Rainier was the nation's fifth national park. It was the first national park to allow cars. Managing parking, traffic, and road use have been a challenge to manage while ensuring the wilderness stays wild.

This park gets about two million visitors every year. It is a popular place to hike and camp in the summertime. People travel from all over the world to see and photograph the summer meadows filled with wildflowers. In spring and winter, visitors can also snowshoe and see glaciers up close.

Mount Rainier is famous for:
- glaciers
- sub-alpine meadows
- beautiful wildflowers

Hey! I'm Parker!

I'm the only snail in history to visit every National Park in the United States! Come join me on my adventures in Mount Rainier National Park.

Throughout this book, we will learn about the history of the park, the animals and plants that live here, and things to do if you ever visit in person. This book is also full of games and activities!

Last but not least, I am hidden 9 times on different pages. See how many times you can find me. This page doesn't count!

Mount Rainier Bingo

Let's play bingo! Cross off each box you are able to during your visit to the national park. Try to get a bingo down, across, or diagonally. If you can't visit the park, use the bingo board to plan your perfect trip.

Pick out some activities you would want to do during your visit. What would you do first? How long would you spend there? What animals would you try to see?

SPOT A SALAMANDER	SEE A GLACIER	IDENTIFY A TREE	TAKE A PICTURE AT AN OVERLOOK	WATCH A MOVIE AT THE VISITORS CENTER
GO FOR A HIKE	LEARN ABOUT THE INDIGENOUS PEOPLE WHO LIVE IN THIS AREA	WITNESS A SUNRISE OR SUNSET	OBSERVE THE NIGHT SKIES	GO SNOWSHOEING
HEAR A BIRD CALL	VISIT PARADISE	FREE SPACE	LEARN ABOUT THE IMPORTANCE OF THE SALMON	VISIT A RANGER STATION
PICK UP A PIECE OF TRASH	GO CAMPING	SEE AN ELK	VISIT LONGMIRE	SPOT A BIRD OF PREY
LEARN ABOUT THE GEOLOGY OF THE MOUNTAIN	SEE THE COLUMNAR LAVA	HAVE A PICNIC	SPOT SOME ANIMAL TRACKS	PARTICIPATE IN A RANGER-LED ACTIVITY

Take a Hike

Go for a hike with your friends or family. If you aren't able to visit Mount Rainier National Park, go for a walk in a park near where you live. Read through the prompts before your walk and finish the activities after you return.

Draw something you saw that moves:

Draw something you saw when you looked up:

Draw something you saw that grows out of the ground:

Draw a picture of your favorite part of the walk:

Things to Do Jumble

Unscramble the letters to uncover activities you can do while in Mount Rainier National Park. Hint: each one ends in -ing.

1. BTOA
   ☐☐☐☐ ING

2. IHK
   ☐☐☐ ING

3. DBIR
   ☐☐☐☐ ING

4. MACP
   ☐☐☐☐ ING

5. KINICPC
   ☐☐☐☐☐☐☐ ING

6. EISSTEHG
   ☐☐☐☐☐☐☐☐ ING

7. SHOSNOWE
   ☐☐☐☐☐☐☐☐ ING

Word Bank

birding

reading

camping

snowshoeing

horseback riding

hiking

rock climbing

singing

boating

sightseeing

picnicking

The National Park Logo

The National Park System has over 400 units in the US. Just like Mount Rainier National Park, each location is unique or special in some way. The areas include other national parks, historic sites, monuments, seashores, and other recreation areas.

Each element of the National Park emblem represents something that the National Park Service protects. Fill in each blank below to show what each symbol represents.

```
WORD BANK:
_____
MOUNTAINS, ARROWHEAD, BISON,
SEQUOIA TREE, WATER
```

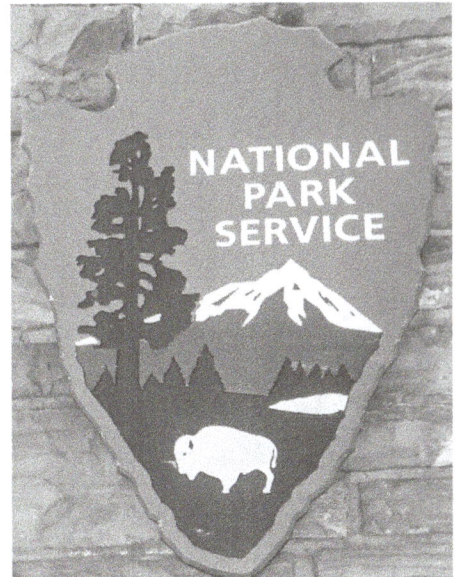

This represents all plants: _____

This represents all animals: _____

This represents the landscapes: _____

This represents the waters protected by the park service: _____

This represents the historical and archeological values: _____

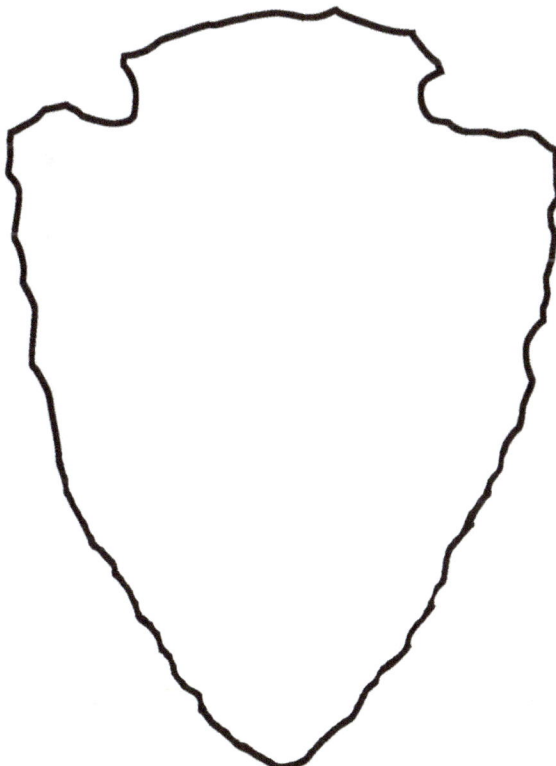

Now it's your turn! Pretend you are designing a new national park. Add elements to the design that represent the things your park protects

What is the name of your park?

Describe why you included the symbols you included. What do they mean?

Go Birdwatching at Paradise

start here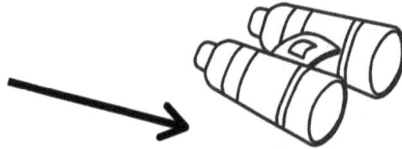

Camping Packing List

What should you take with you when you go camping? Pretend you are in charge of your family camping trip. Make a list of what you would need to be safe and comfortable on an overnight excursion. Some considerations are listed on the side.

1.
2.
3.
4.
5.
6.
7.
8.
9.
10.
11.
12.
13.
14.
15.
16.

- What will you eat at every meal?

- What will the weather be like?

- Where will you sleep?

- What will you do during your free time?

- How luxurious do you want camp to be?

- How will you cook?

- How will you see at night?

- How will you dispose of trash?

- What might you need in case of emergencies?

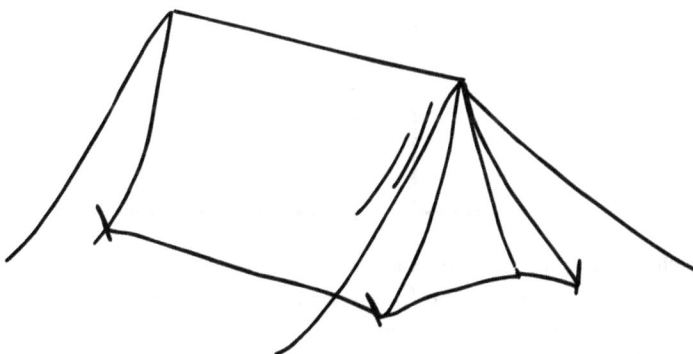

Mount Rainier National Park

Date:

Season:

Who I went with:

Which entrance:

How was your experience? Write a few sentences about your trip. Where did you stay? What did you do? What was your favorite activity? If you haven't visited the park yet, write a paragraph pretending that you did.

STAMPS

Many national parks and monuments have cancellation stamps for visitors to use. These rubber stamps record the date and location that you visited. Many people collect the markings as a free souvenir. Check with a ranger to see where you can find a stamp during your visit. If you aren't able to find one, you can draw your own.

Where is the Park?

Mount Rainier National Park is in the northwest United States. It is located in Washington State. Don't confuse it with Washington, D.C., which is located on the other side of the country!

Washington

Look at the shape of Washington. Can you find it on the map? If you are from the US, can you find your home state? Color Washington red. Put a star on the map where you live.

Connect the Dots #1

Connect the dots to figure out what this tiny critter is. There are two types of these that live in Mount Rainier National Park.

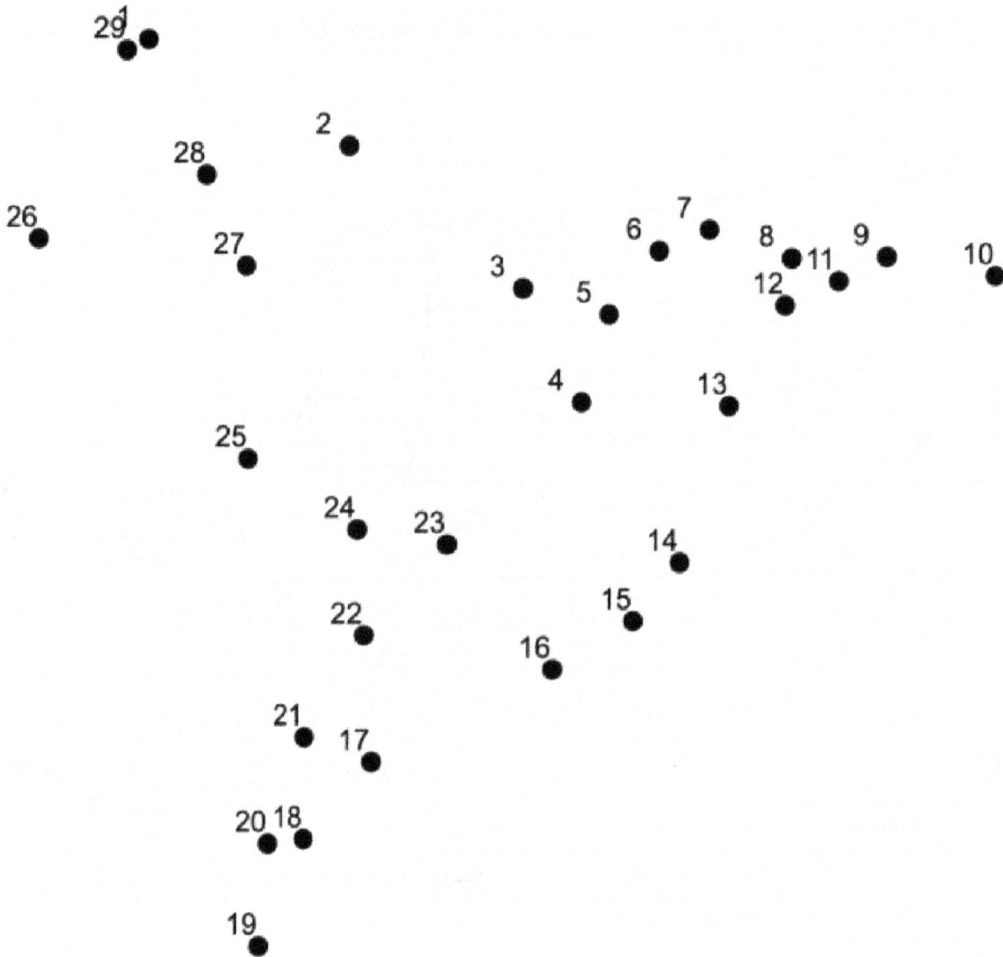

1
29
2
28
26
7
6
27
8
9
3
11
10
5
12
4
13
25
24
23
14
15
22
16
21
17
20 18
19

Their heart rate can reach as high as 1,260 beats per minute and a breathing rate of 250 breaths per minute. Have you ever measured your breathing rate? Ask a friend or family member to set a timer for 60 seconds. Once they say "go," try to breathe normally. Count each breath until they say "stop." How do your breaths per minute compare to hummingbirds?

_____

_____

Pikas are related to rabbits, but they have distinctly rounded ears. They can be hard to spot but you might hear them. Listen for their short, high-pitched call.

Mountain lions, also known as cougars, are rarely seen by humans. They favor remote forested places in the park.

Who Lives Here?

Below are 12 plants and animals that live in the park.
Use the word bank to fill in the clues below.

word bank: pika, huckleberry, grand fir, elk, mink, mountain lion, beaver, coyote, tiger lily, bobcat, porcupine, paintbrush

M □ □ □

□ O □ □ □ □

□ U □ □ □ □ □ □ □ □ □ □

□ □ □ □ □ □ □ □ N ■ □ □ □ □

□ □ □ □ T □

□ □ R □ □ □ □ □

□ A □ □ □ □ □ □ □

□ I □ □

□ □ □ N □ ■ □ □

□ □ □ □ □ ■ □ I □ □

E □ □

□ □ □ □ □ R

14

Porcupines are well known for their defense mechanism, their quills! If attacked, these quills easily detach from the porcupine's back to pierce potential predators.

Beavers are the largest North American rodent. At Mount Rainier National Park, look for them around the Longmire Meadow.

Common Names
vs.
Scientific Names

A common name of an organism is a name that is based on everyday language. You have heard the common names of plants, animals, and other living things on tv, in books, and at school. Common names can also be referred to as "English" names, popular names, or farmer's names. Common names can vary from place to place. The word for a particular tree may be one thing, but that same tree has a different name in another country. Common names can even vary from region to region, even in the same country.

Scientific names, or Latin names, are given to organisms to make it possible to have uniform names for the same species. Scientific names are in Latin. You may have heard plants or animals referred to by their scientific name or parts of their scientific names. Latin names are also called "binomial nomenclature," which refers to a two-part naming system. The first part of the name – the generic name – refers to the genus to which the species belongs. The second part of the name, the specific name, identifies the species. For example, Tyrannosaurus rex is an example of a widely known scientific name.

American Black Bear

Ursus americanus

COMMON NAME

Elk

Cervus canadensis

LATIN NAME = GENUS + SPECIES

Elk = Cervus canadensis

Black Bear = Ursus americanus

Find the Match!
Common Names and Latin Names

Match the common name to the scientific name for each animal. The first one is done for you. Use clues on the page before and after this one to complete the matches.

Elk	Haliaeetus leucocephalus
Cascade Huckleberry	Ursus americanus
Western Red Cedar	Lagopus leucura
American Black Bear	Ochotona princeps
Great Horned Owl	Vaccinium deliciosum
Bald Eagle	Charina bottae
Ptarmigan	Bubo virginianus
Pika	Cervus canadensis
Rubber Boa	Thuja plicata

Bald Eagle

Haliaeetus leucocephalus

Ptarmigan
Lagopus leucura

Bald Eagle
Haliaeetus leucocephalus

Great Horned Owl
Bubo virginianus

Some plants and animals that live at Mount Rainier

Cascade Huckleberry
Vaccinium deliciosum

Pika
Ochotona princeps

Rubber Boa
Charina bottae

The Ten Essentials

Careful preparation and knowledge are key to a successful adventure into Mount Rainier National Park's backcountry.

The ten essentials are a list of things that are important to have when you go for longer hikes. If you go on a hike in the <u>backcountry</u>, it is especially important that you have everything you need in case of an emergency. If you get lost or something unforeseen happens, it is good to be prepared to survive until help finds you.

The ten essentials list was developed in the 1930s by an outdoors group called the Mountaineers. Over time and technological advancements, this list has evolved. Can you identify all the things on the current list? Circle each of the "essentials" and cross out everything that doesn't make the cut.

fire: matches, lighter, tinder, and/or stove	a pint of milk	extra money	headlamp, plus extra batteries	extra clothes
extra water	a dog	Polaroid camera	bug net	lightweight games, like a deck of cards
extra food	a roll of duct tape	shelter	sun protection, such as sunglasses, sun-protective clothes, and sunscreen	knife, plus a gear repair kit
a mirror	navigation: map, compass, altimeter, GPS device, or satellite messenger	first aid kit	extra flip-flops	entertainment, such as video games or books

Backcountry - a remote, undeveloped rural area.

Photobook

Draw some pictures of
things you saw in the park.

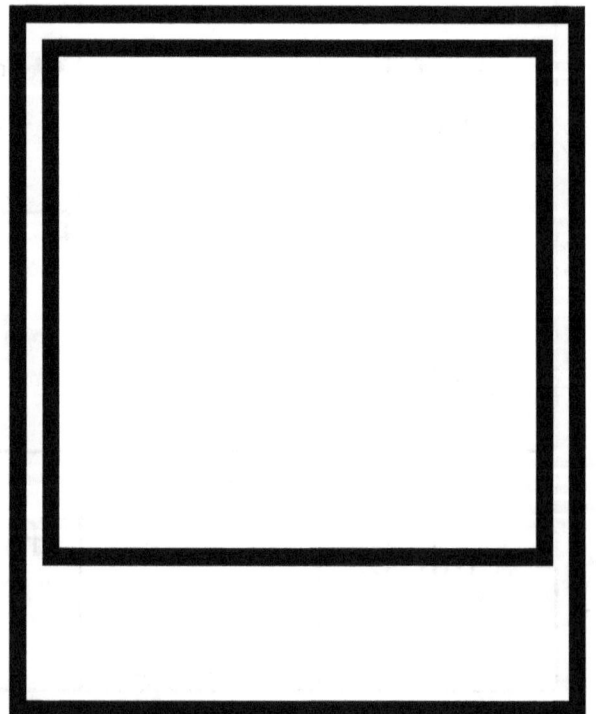

Connect the Dots #2

This animal lives in almost every state in the US, including the national park. They are nocturnal, more active at night, and sleep during the day. They are omnivorous eaters, meaning they eat both plants and animals.

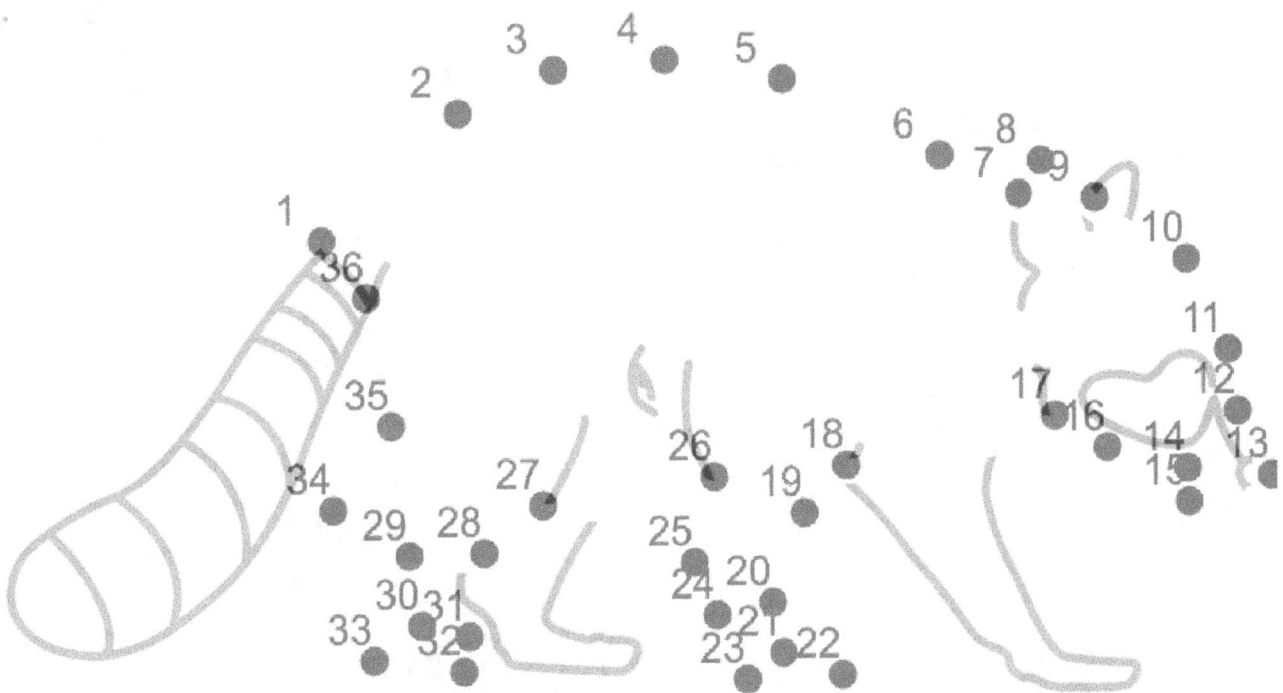

Are you an omnivore like a raccoon? An herbivore only eats plant foods. A carnivore only eats meat. An omnivore eats both. What type of eater are you? Write down some of your favorite foods to back up your answer.

_____

_____

LISTEN CAREFULLY

Visitors to Mount Rainier National Park may hear different noises from those they hear at home. Try this activity to experience this for yourself!

First, find a place outside where it is comfortable to sit or stand for a few minutes. You can do this by yourself or with a friend or family member. Once you have a good spot, close your eyes and listen. Be quiet for one minute and pay attention to what you are hearing. List some of the sounds you have heard in one of the two boxes below:

NATURAL SOUNDS
MADE BY ANIMALS, TREES OR PLANTS, THE WIND, ETC

HUMAN-MADE SOUNDS
MADE BY PEOPLE, MACHINES, ETC

ONCE YOU ARE BACK AT HOME, TRY REPEATING YOUR EXPERIMENT:

NATURAL SOUNDS
MADE BY ANIMALS, TREES OR PLANTS, THE WIND, ETC

HUMAN-MADE SOUNDS
MADE BY PEOPLE, MACHINES, ETC

WHERE DID YOU HEAR MORE NATURAL SOUNDS?

WHERE DID YOU HEAR MORE HUMAN SOUNDS?

Mount Rainier
Word Search

Words may be horizontal, vertical, diagonal,
or they might even be backwards!

1. glacier
2. ridge
3. peak
4. volcano
5. lakes
6. Cascade
7. entrance
8. Tahoma
9. wildflowers
10. climbers
11. Paradise
12. Longmire
13. snowshoe
14. salmon
15. marmots
16. ferns
17. Aurora Lake
18. Nisqually
19. Puyallup
20. meadow

```
C W I L D F L O W E R S A O K
H T P E A K O E S H E R N R J
T E P O K A N O C C L A A P B
S M P H S P G U C A C L U M C
P E A S A L M O N L I U J K L
U O L W Y W I O O A T E A C I
Y E A O A R R V C P B R I A M
A C C N M L E N T A H O M A B
L N H S E E L O E E S D S P E
L A I C A B O Y G L A C I E R
U R A H D C M C D N M E A C S
P T N I O M O A I M O K I D I
I N O S W O I S R J R A Q N E
O E G T L E V E S M S R V E F
N I S Q U A L L Y E O O H E E
X J T F I R E F K I E T Q N R
U E S I D A R A P E T P S E N
A U R O R A L A K E M A L A S
```

Find the Match!
What are Baby Animals Called?

Match the animal to its baby. The first one is done for you.

Elk	eaglet
Bald Eagle	calf
Little Brown Bat	snakelets
Striped Skunk	pup
Great Horned Owl	owlet
Western Toad	kit
Mountain Lion	tadpole
Garter snake	kitten

The Perfect Picnic Spot

Fill in the blanks on this page without looking at the full story. Once you have each line filled out, use the words you've chosen to complete the story on the next page.

EMOTION _____

FOOD _____

SOMETHING SWEET _____

STORE _____

MODE OF TRANSPORTATION _____

NOUN _____

SOMETHING ALIVE _____

SAUCE _____

PLURAL VEGETABLES _____

ADJECTIVE _____

PLURAL BODY PART _____

ANIMAL _____

PLURAL FRUIT _____

PLACE _____

SOMETHING TALL _____

COLOR _____

ADJECTIVE _____

NOUN _____

A DIFFERENT ANIMAL _____

FAMILY MEMBER #1 _____

FAMILY MEMBER #2 _____

VERB THAT ENDS IN -ING _____

A DIFFERENT FOOD _____

The Perfect Picnic Spot

Use the words from the previous page to complete a silly story.

When my family suggested having our lunch at the Sunrise picnic area, I was

_____. I love eating my _____ outside! I knew we had picked up a
EMOTION   FOOD

box of _____ from the _____ for after lunch, my favorite. We drove up
SOMETHING SWEET   STORE

to the area and I jumped out of the _____. "I will find the perfect spot for
                   MODE OF TRANSPORTATION

a picnic!" I grabbed a _____ for us to sit on, and I ran off. I passed a picnic
            NOUN

table, but it was covered with _____ so we couldn't sit there. The next
                 SOMETHING ALIVE

picnic table looked okay, but there were smears of _____ and pieces of
                                   SAUCE

_____ everywhere. The people that were there before must have been
PLURAL VEGETABLES

_____! I gritted my _____ together and kept walking down the path,
ADJECTIVE   PLURAL BODY PART

determined to find the perfect spot. I wanted a table with a good view of the

glacier. Why was this so hard? If we were lucky, I might even get to see _____
                                        ANIMAL

eating some _____ on the cliffside. They don't have those in _____ where I
         PLURAL FRUIT   PLACE

am from. I walked down a little hill and there it was, the perfect spot! The trees

towered overhead and looked as tall as _____. The patch of grass was a
                                SOMETHING TALL

beautiful _____ color. The _____ flowers were growing on
          COLOR   ADJECTIVE

the side of a _____. I looked across the glacier edge and even saw a
          NOUN

_____ on the edge of a rock. I looked back to see my _____ and
DIFFERENT ANIMAL   FAMILY MEMBER #1

_____ _____ a picnic basket. "I hope you brought plenty of
FAMILY MEMBER #2   VERB THAT ENDS IN ING

_____, I'm starving!"
A DIFFERENT FOOD

27

Wildlife Wisdom

The national park is home to many different kinds of animals. Seeing wildlife can be an exciting part of visiting the national park but it is important to remember that these animals are wild. They need plenty of space and a healthy habitat where they can find their own food. Part of this is not allowing animals to eat any human food. This is their home and we are the visitors. We need to be respectful of the wildlife in the park.

Directions: Circle the highlighted words that best complete the following sentences.

If an animal changes its behavior because of your presence, you are:
  A) too close
  B) funny looking
  C) dehydrated and should drink more water

The best thing we can do to help wild animals survive is:
  A) make them pets
  B) protect their habitat
  C) knit them winter sweaters

In a national park, it is okay to share your food with wild animals:
  A) never
  B) always
  C) sometimes

When you're hiking in an area where there are bears, you should warn bears that you are entering their space by:
  A) hiking quietly
  B) making noise
  C) wearing bright colors

At night, park rangers care for the animals by:
  A) putting them back into their cages
  B) tucking them into bed
  C) leaving them alone

If you see an abandoned bird's nest, it is best to:
  A) pet the baby birds
  B) leave it alone
  C) crunch the empty eggshells

Bears look under logs in hopes of finding:
  A) granola bars
  B) insects
  C) peanuts to eat

The place where an animal lives is called its:
  A) condo
  B) habitat
  C) crib

Design a Water Bottle

Imagine you've been hired to design a reusable water bottle that will be for sale in the national park gift shop. It will be a souvenir for visitors to remember their trip to the park.

Consider adding a plant or animal that lives here, or include a famous place in the park or activity that you can do while visiting.

Hike to a Glacier

start here

DID YOU KNOW?
There are 25 glaciers in Mount Rainier National Park.

Glaciers of Mount Rainier
Word Search

Glaciers are huge masses of ice that "flow" like slow rivers. They form over hundreds of years where fallen snow compresses and turns into ice. Mount Rainier has 25 glaciers. Can you find some?

1. Carbon
2. Cowlitz
3. Edmunds
4. Emmons
5. Flett
6. Inter
7. Kautz
8. Nisqually
9. Ohanapecosh
10. Paradise
11. Puyallup
12. Pyramid
13. Russell
14. Sarvant
15. Success
16. Whitman
17. Wilson
18. Winthrop

```
C W E M M O N S E S K L O W K
H O D T M I L Z S H E R W R N
T H M R K I N T E R P B A O B
S A U A S P R U C E U L B M S
C N N I S Q U A L L Y R J K U
A A D D Y W O K D B A E A C C
R P S D P R E G A C L R I A C
P E B A M E I N W I L S O N E
R C H P G E L O B E U D S P S
E O I R Y B O Y H I P G O T S
Q S A U A R I C N N E E N C N
S H N S K W A I S M S K I R E
I J O S F H I M Z T I L W O C
J Y G E L I V E I O D R V E O
N W X L K T A B E D A O H E M
T T E L F M E G S A R V A N T
U A E E S A E N N E A P V E B
C J D W I N T H R O P A L A S
```

Leave No Trace Quiz

Leave No Trace is a concept that helps people make decisions during outdoor recreation that protects the environment. There are seven principles that guide us when we spend time outdoors, whether you are in a national park or not. Are you an expert in Leave No Trace? Take this quiz and find out!

1. How can you plan ahead and prepare to ensure you have the best experience you can in the national park?
    a. Make sure you stop by the ranger station for a map and to ask about current conditions.
    b. Just wing it! You will know the best trail when you see it.
    c. Stick to your plan, even if conditions change. You traveled a long way to get here, and you should stick to your plan.
2. What is an example of traveling on a durable surface?
    a. Walking only on the designated path.
    b. Walking on the grass that borders the trail if the trail is very muddy.
    c. Taking a shortcut if you can find one because it means you will be walking less.
3. Why should you dispose of waste properly?
    a. You don't need to. Park rangers love to pick up the trash you leave behind.
    b. You should actually leave your leftovers behind, because animals will eat them. It is important to make sure they aren't hungry.
    c. So that other peoples' experiences of the park are not impacted by you leaving your waste behind.
4. How can you best follow the concept "leave what you find?"
    a. Take only a small rock or leaf to remember your trip.
    b. Take pictures, but leave any physical items where they are.
    c. Leave everything you find, unless it may be rare like an arrowhead, then it is okay to take.
5. What is not a good example of minimizing campfire impacts?
    a. Only having a campfire in a pre-existing campfire ring.
    b. Checking in with current conditions when you consider making a campfire.
    c. Building a new campfire ring in a location that has a better view.
6. What is a poor example of respecting wildlife?
    a. Building squirrel houses out of rocks so the squirrels have a place to live.
    b. Stay far away from wildlife and give them plenty of space.
    c. Reminding your grown-ups not to drive too fast in animal habitats while visiting the park.
7. How can you show consideration of other visitors?
    a. Play music on your speaker so other people at the campground can enjoy it.
    b. Wear headphones on the trail if you choose to listen to music.
    c. Make sure to yell "Hello!" to every animal you see at top volume.

Park Poetry

America's parks inspire art of all kinds. Painters, sculptors, photographers, writers, and artists of all mediums have taken inspiration from natural beauty. They have turned their inspiration into great works.

Use this space to write your own poem about the park. Think about what you have experienced or seen. Use descriptive language to create an acrostic poem. This type of poem has the first letter of each line spell out another word. Create an acrostic that spells out the word "Volcano."

V _____

O _____

L _____

C _____

A _____

N _____

O _____

Very
Old
Landscape
Curves
And
Nature
Overrun

Visiting
Our Mountain
Low to high
Countryside to forests
And we drove
Now at the top
On top of the world

Catch a Fish in the Nisqually River

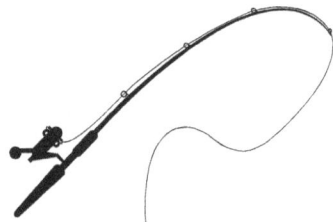

start here

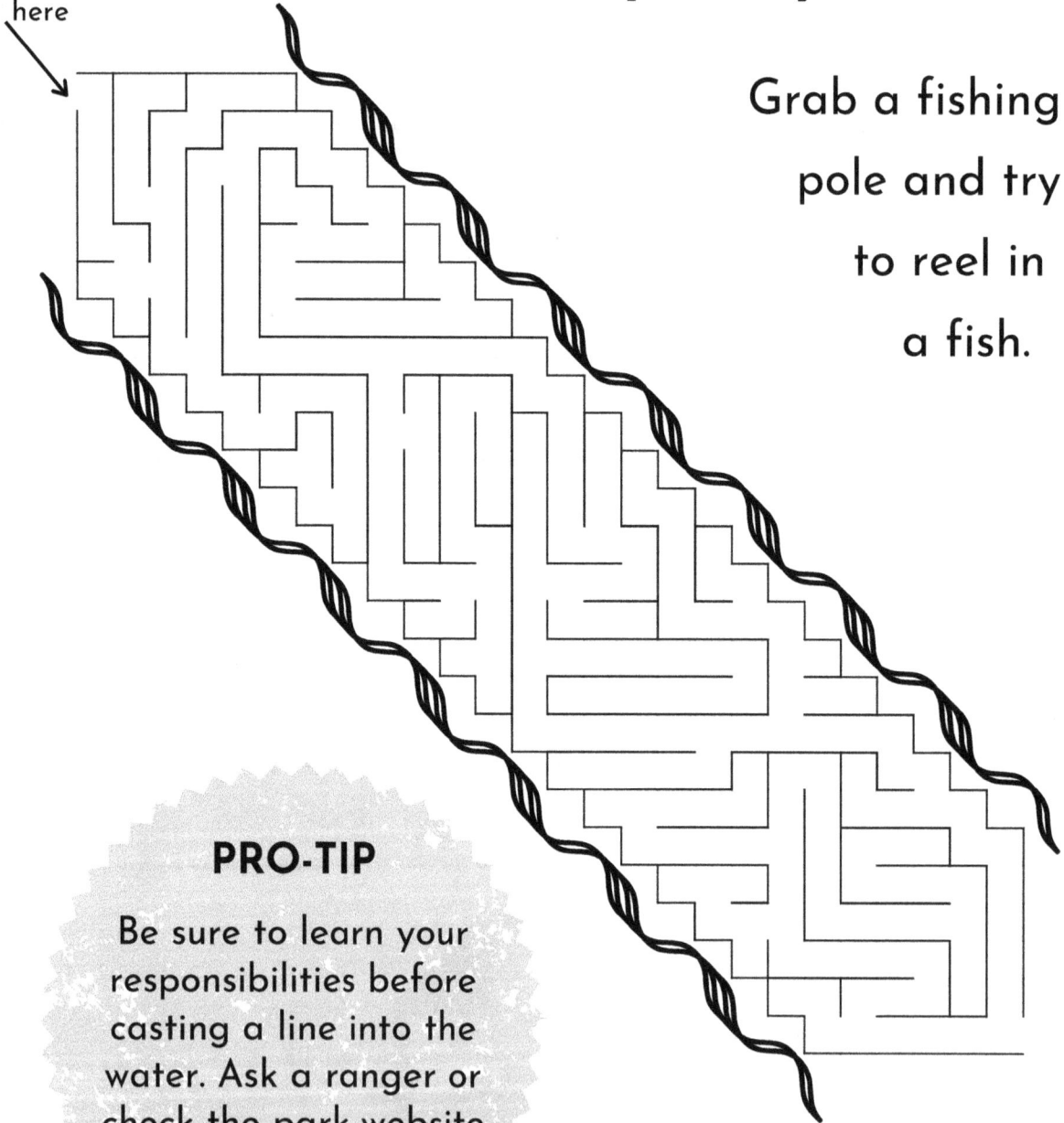

Grab a fishing pole and try to reel in a fish.

PRO-TIP

Be sure to learn your responsibilities before casting a line into the water. Ask a ranger or check the park website before you go.

34

Stacking Rocks

Have you ever seen stacks of rocks while hiking in national parks? Do you know what they are or what they mean? These rock piles are called cairns and often mark hiking routes in parks. Every park has a different way to maintain trails and cairns. However, they all have the same rule: If you come across a cairn, do not disturb it!

Color the cairn and the rules to remember.

1. Do not tamper with cairns.

If a cairn is tampered with or an unauthorized one is built, then future visitors may become disoriented or even lost.

2. Do not build unauthorized cairns.

Moving rocks disturbs the soil and makes the area more prone to erosion. Disturbing rocks can disturb fragile plants.

3. Do not add to existing cairns.

Authorized cairns are carefully designed. Adding to them can actually cause them to collapse.

Crack the Code

Use the code to figure out some fun facts about Mount Rainier National Park.

ANSWER: A B C D E F G H I J K L M N O P Q R S T U V W Y

CODE: O T D A J K E F Y L R Q S W I G N H P U V M C B

What is the most visited glacier in the park?

_ _ _ _ _ _ _ _ _
W Y P N V O Q Q B

Mount Rainier is the tallest mountain in this mountain range.

_ _ _ _ _ _ _
D O P D O A J

Seismological research happens at Mount Rainier. What is seismology the study of?

_ _ _ _ _ _ _ _ _ _ _
J O H U F N V O R J P

The Land of the Puyallup

There are six tribes that have connections to the lands and resources found within the current boundaries of Mount Rainier National Park. The Puyallup Tribe is just one of those groups. The Tribe has a reservation to the northeast of the mountain. Complete the crossword puzzle below to learn more about the Puyallup people.

Word Bank

TAHOMA
URBAN
CULTURE
WASHINGTON
MEDICINE CREEK
FISHING
BERRY-PICKING
LUSHOOTSEED
ART
POTLATCH
CEDAR

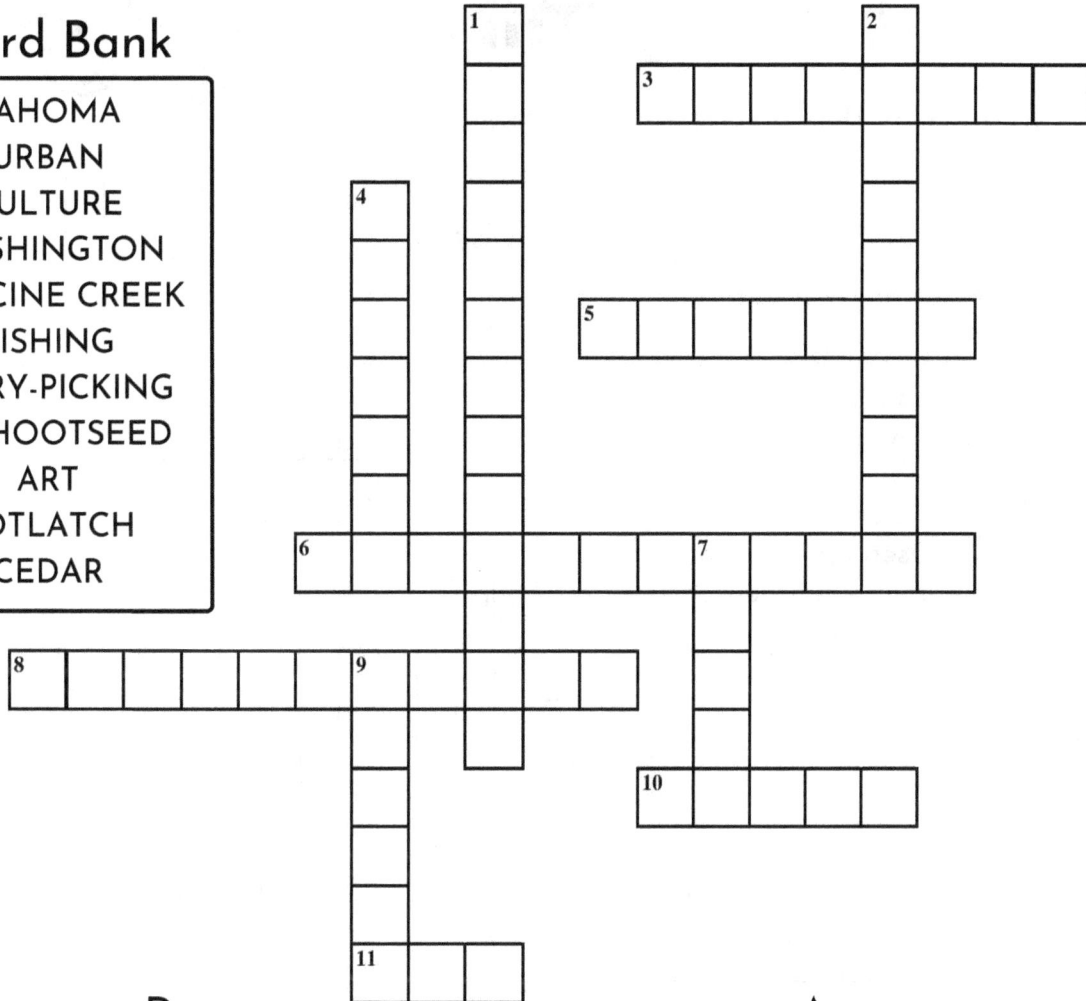

Down

1. The treaty that the US government created to take land away from the Puyallup and neighboring tribes.

2. Modern-day state where many Puyallup People live.

4. This is ever-evolving and includes the customs, arts, social institutions, and achievements of a people group.

7. A type of tree important to Puyallup life used to make clothing, homes, and canoes.

9. A Puyallup name for Mount Rainier.

Across

3. A traditional event that centers around gift-giving, food, song, storytelling, and gathering.

5. An important traditional and cultural activity related to food.

6. Gathering of blackberries, salmonberries, and other berries.

8. The Puyallup people traditionally spoke a dialect of this language. Many speak it today.

10. The Puyallup reservation is this, meaning much of their land is within a city-like environment.

11. Creative activities that express imaginative or technical skill. It produces a product, an object.

Go Snowshoeing at Longmire

Help find Parker's winter hat!

start here →

DID YOU KNOW?

Snowshoes help you walk on the snow. They distribute your weight so that you almost float on the surface of the snow. They have been used for thousands of years around the world.

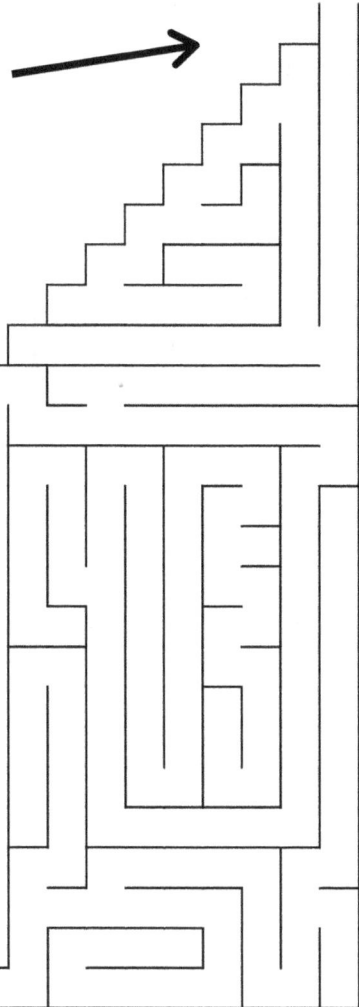

Butterflies of the Cascades

Dozens of species of butterflies and moths live in Mount Rainier National Park. Their wingspan size varies, as do the patterns on their wings. Design your own butterfly below. Make sure the wings are symmetrical, which means both sides match.

A Hike at Mount Rainier

Fill in the blanks on this page without looking at the full story. Once you have each line filled out, use the words you've chosen to complete the story on the next page.

ADJECTIVE _____

SOMETHING TO EAT _____

SOMETHING TO DRINK _____

NOUN _____

ARTICLE OF CLOTHING _____

BODY PART _____

VERB _____

ANIMAL _____

SAME TYPE OF FOOD _____

ADJECTIVE _____

SAME ANIMAL _____

VERB THAT ENDS IN "ED" _____

NUMBER _____

A DIFFERENT NUMBER _____

SOMETHING THAT FLIES _____

LIGHT SOURCE _____

PLURAL NOUN _____

FAMILY MEMBER _____

YOUR NICKNAME _____

A Hike at Mount Rainier

Use the words from the previous page to complete a silly story.

I went for a hike at Mount Rainier today. In my favorite _____ backpack,
ADJECTIVE

I made sure to pack a map so I wouldn't get lost. I also threw in an extra

_____ just in case I got hungry and a bottle of _____. I put
SOMETHING TO EAT   SOMETHING TO DRINK

on my _____ spray, and I tied a _____ around my
NOUN   ARTICLE OF CLOTHING

_____, in case it gets chilly. I started to _____ down the path. As
BODY PART   VERB

soon as I turned the corner, I came face to face with a(n) _____. I think
ANIMAL

it was as startled as I was! What should I do? I had to think fast! Should I

give it some of my _____? No. I had to remember what the
SAME TYPE OF FOOD

_____ ranger told me: "If you see one, back away slowly and try not to
ADJECTIVE

scare it." Soon enough, the _____ _____ away. The coast
SAME ANIMAL   VERB THAT ENDS IN ED

was clear. _____ hours later, I finally got to the lookout. I felt like I could
NUMBER

see for a _____ miles. I took a picture of a _____ so I could always
A DIFFERENT NUMBER   NOUN

remember this moment. As I was putting my camera away, a _____
SOMETHING THAT FLIES

flew by, reminding me that it was almost nighttime. I turned on my

_____ and headed back. I could hear the _____ singing their
LIGHT SOURCE   PLURAL INSECT

evening song. Just as I was getting tired, I saw my _____ and our tent.
FAMILY MEMBER

"Welcome back _____! How was your hike?"
NICKNAME

41

Let's Go Camping Word Search

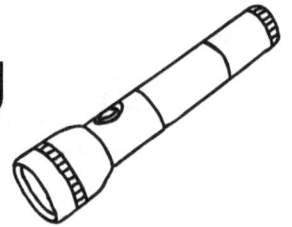

Words may be horizontal, vertical, diagonal, or they might even be backwards!

1. tent
2. camp stove
3. sleeping bag
4. bug spray
5. sunscreen
6. map
7. flashlight
8. pillow
9. lantern
10. ice
11. snacks
12. smores
13. water
14. first aid kit
15. chair
16. cards
17. books
18. games
19. trail
20. hat

```
D P P I L L O W D B T E A C I
E O A D P R E A A M B R C A N
P W C A M P S T O V E I H X G
R A H S G E L E B E E D A P S
E L B U G S P R A Y N G I E A
S I A H G C I C N N M E R C N
C W N L A F I R S K O O B F K
M T A E M I L E L H M R W L J
T A P R E A O R E S L B A A B
S M P A S R R T E N T L U S C
C E A I I R C G P E I U J H A
S S N A C K S S I M O K I L R
I J R S F O I S N J R A Q I D
C Y E T L E V E G U O R V G S
E W T A K C A B B S S O H H M
X J N F I R S T A I D K I T T
U A A E S S E N G E T P V A B
C J L I A R T D N A M A H A S
```

42

All in the Day of a Park Ranger

Park Rangers are hardworking individuals dedicated to protecting our parks, monuments, museums, and more. They take care of the natural and cultural resources for future generations. Rangers also help protect the visitors of the park. Their responsibilities are broad and they work both with the public and behind the scenes.

What have you seen park rangers do? Use your knowledge of the duties of park rangers to fill out a typical daily schedule, listing one activity for each hour. Feel free to make up your own, but some examples of activities are provided on the right. Read carefully! Not all the example activities are befitting a ranger.

6 am	Lead a sunrise hike
7 am	
8 am	
9 am	
10 am	
11 am	
12 pm	Enjoy a lunch break outside
1 pm	
2 pm	
3 pm	
4 pm	Teach visitors about the geology of the mountain
5 pm	
6 pm	
7 pm	
8 pm	
9 pm	

- feed a bald eagles
- build trails for visitors to enjoy
- throw rocks off the side of the mountain
- rescue lost hikers
- study animal behavior
- record air quality data
- answer questions at the visitor center
- pick wildflowers
- pick up litter
- share marshmallows with squirrels
- repair handrails
- lead a class on a field trip
- catch frogs and make them race
- lead people on educational hikes
- write articles for the park website
- protect the river from pollution
- remove non-native plants from the park
- study how climate change is affecting the park
- give a talk about mountain lions
- lead a program for campers on volcanoes

If you were a park ranger, which of the above tasks would you enjoy most?

_____

_____

Draw Yourself
as a Park Ranger

RANGER

_____

The Fish of Mount Rainier

1.

ITWHISFWH

Unscramble the common names of these fish that live in the park.

2.

OTRTU

3.

LASNOM

4.

SPINLUC

5.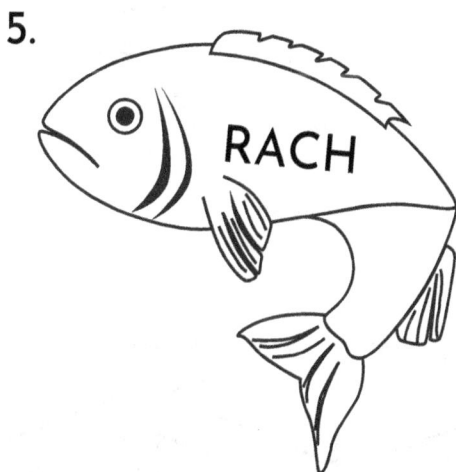

RACH

1. _____
2. _____
3. _____
4. _____
5. _____

Word Bank

salmon
sunfish
trout
minnow
sculpin
char
whitefish
catfish

Amphibians

One species of toad and four species of frogs live at Mount Rainier. Even more types of salamanders live there too. Frogs and toads both spend the beginning of their lives the same way - as tadpoles. Tadpoles hatch from eggs, usually in springs or pools of water.

Both frogs and toads are amphibians. Salamanders are amphibians too. Color the amphibians below.

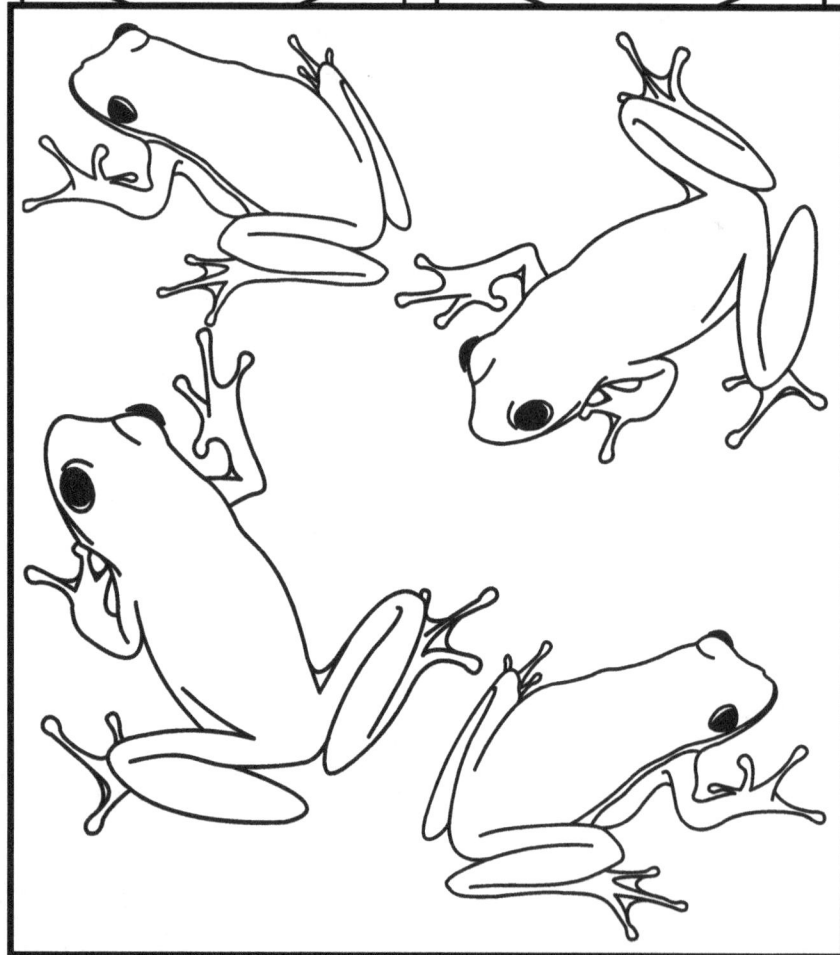

Field Notes

Spend some time reflecting on your trip to Mount Rainier National Park. Your field notes will help you remember the things you experienced. Use the space below to write about your day.

While I was at Mount Rainier National Park...

I saw:

_____

_____

_____

_____

_____

I heard:

_____

_____

_____

_____

I felt:

_____

_____   Draw a picture of your
_____   favorite thing in the park.

I wondered:

_____

_____

_____

_____

63 National Parks

How many other national parks have you been to? Which one do you want to visit next? Note that if some of these parks fall on the border of more than one state, you may check it off more than once!

Alaska
- ☐ Denali National Park
- ☐ Gates of the Arctic National Park
- ☐ Glacier Bay National Park
- ☐ Katmai National Park
- ☐ Kenai Fjords National Park
- ☐ Kobuk Valley National Park
- ☐ Lake Clark National Park
- ☐ Wrangell-St. Elias National Park

American Samoa
- ☐ National Park of American Samoa

Arizona
- ☐ Grand Canyon National Park
- ☐ Petrified Forest National Park
- ☐ Saguaro National Park

Arkansas
- ☐ Hot Springs National Park

California
- ☐ Channel Islands National Park
- ☐ Death Valley National Park
- ☐ Joshua Tree National Park
- ☐ Kings Canyon National Park
- ☐ Lassen Volcanic National Park
- ☐ Pinnacles National Park
- ☐ Redwood National Park
- ☐ Sequoia National Park
- ☐ Yosemite National Park

Colorado
- ☐ Black Canyon of the Gunnison National Park
- ☐ Great Sand Dunes National Park
- ☐ Mesa Verde National Park
- ☐ Rocky Mountain National Park

Florida
- ☐ Biscayne National Park
- ☐ Dry Tortugas National Park
- ☐ Everglades National Park

Hawaii
- ☐ Haleakalā National Park
- ☐ Hawai'i Volcanoes National Park

Idaho
- ☐ Yellowstone National Park

Kentucky
- ☐ Mammoth Cave National Park

Indiana
- ☐ Indiana Dunes National Park

Maine
- ☐ Acadia National Park

Michigan
- ☐ Isle Royale National Park

Minnesota
- ☐ Voyageurs National Park

Missouri
- ☐ Gateway Arch National Park

Montana
- ☐ Glacier National Park
- ☐ Yellowstone National Park

Nevada
- ☐ Death Valley National Park
- ☐ Great Basin National Park

New Mexico
- ☐ Carlsbad Caverns National Park
- ☐ White Sands National Park

North Dakota
- ☐ Theodore Roosevelt National Park

North Carolina
- ☐ Great Smoky Mountains National Park

Ohio
- ☐ Cuyahoga Valley National Park

Oregon
- ☐ Crater Lake National Park

South Carolina
- ☐ Congaree National Park

South Dakota
- ☐ Badlands National Park
- ☐ Wind Cave National Park

Tennessee
- ☐ Great Smoky Mountains National Park

Texas
- ☐ Big Bend National Park
- ☐ Guadalupe Mountains National Park

Utah
- ☐ Arches National Park
- ☐ Bryce Canyon National Park
- ☐ Canyonlands National Park
- ☐ Capitol Reef National Park
- ☐ Zion National Park

Virgin Islands
- ☐ Virgin Islands National Park

Virginia
- ☐ Shenandoah National Park

Washington
- ☐ Mount Rainier National Park
- ☐ North Cascades National Park
- ☐ Olympic National Park

West Virginia
- ☐ New River Gorge National Park

Wyoming
- ☐ Grand Teton National Park
- ☐ Yellowstone National Park

Other National Parks Crossword

Besides Mount Rainier National Park, there are 62 other diverse and beautiful national parks across the United States. Try your hand at this crossword. If you need help, look at the previous page for some hints.

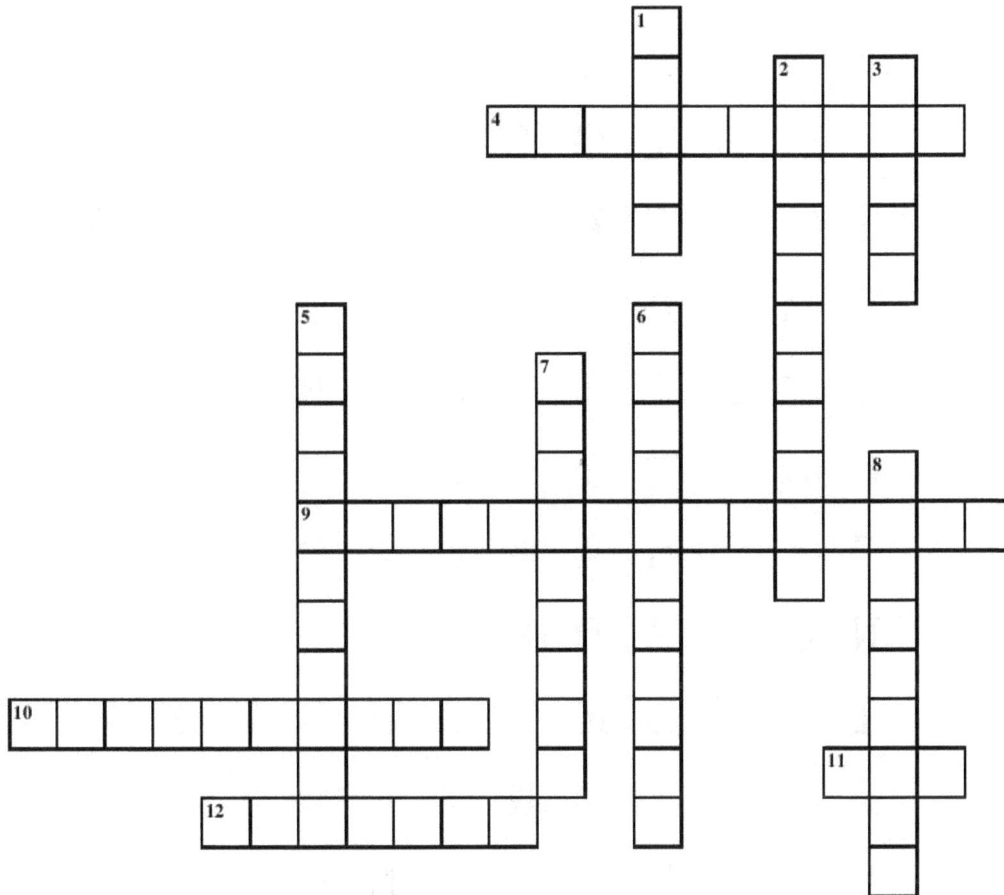

Down

1. State where Acadia National Park is located
2. This national park has the Spanish word for turtle in it
3. Number of national parks in Alaska
5. This national park has some of the hottest temperatures in the world
6. This national park is the only one in Idaho
7. This toothsome creature can famously be found in Everglades National Park
8. Only president with a national park named for them

Across

4. This state has the most national parks.
9. This park has some of the newest land in the US, caused by volcanic eruptions.
10. This park has the deepest lake in the United States.
11. This color shows up in the name of a national park in California.
12. This national park deserves a gold medal.

Which National Park Will You Go to Next?
Word Search

1. Zion
2. Big Bend
3. Glacier
4. Olympic
5. Sequoia
6. Bryce
7. Mesa Verde
8. Biscayne
9. Wind Cave
10. Great Basin
11. Katmai
12. Yellowstone
13. Voyageurs
14. Arches
15. Badlands
16. Denali
17. Glacier Bay
18. Hot Springs

```
F M M E S A V E R D E B N E Y
E A B I G B E N D E S A S E M
Y L I C A L O Y N E E D L T G
D M G A S S A U C N R L U E R
C E L I I T S C R E O A A K E
S N A W Y E E O I W T N A C A
G I C H A A Q C S E M D N S T
N O I Z P R U T I M R S N E B
I W E L M P O N B W E B K H A
R J R F D N I F L I H B U C S
P A B E E S A N E S O P W R I
S J A E N Y A C S I B A U A N
T C Y I A D O H H Y M E A L R
O T A T L M L E S E G R W R J
H S T O I K A T M A I R O P B
I C H U R C O L Y M P I C O U
O Y G T S D E O S B R Y C E T
W I N D C A V E I N R O H E M
```

Bird Scavenger Hunt

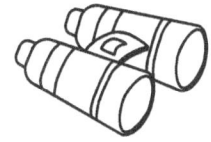

Mount Rainier National Park is a great place to go birdwatching. You don't have to be able to identify different species of birds in order to have fun. Open your eyes and tune in your ears. Check off as many birds on this list as you can.

☐ A colorful bird   ☐ A big bird

☐ A brown bird   ☐ A small bird

☐ A bird in a tree   ☐ A hopping bird

☐ A bird with long tail feathers   ☐ A flying bird

☐ A bird making noise   ☐ A bird's nest

☐ A bird eating or hunting   ☐ A bird's footprint on the ground

☐ A bird with spots   ☐ A bird with stripes somewhere on it

What was the easiest bird on the list to find? What was the hardest?
Why do you think that was?

_____

_____

ANSWER KEY

Jumbles Answers

Unscramble the letters to uncovering activities you can do while in Mount Rainier National Park. Hint: each one ends in -ing.

1. BOATING
2. HIKING
3. BIRDING
4. CAMPING
5. PICNICKING
6. SIGHTSEEING
7. SNOWSHOEING

National Park Emblem Answers

1. This represents all plant: **Sequoia Tree**

2. This represents all animals: **Bison**

3. This symbol represents the landscapes: **Mountains**

4. This represents the waters protected by the park service: **Water**

5. This represents the historical and archeological values: **Arrowhead**

Go Birdwatching at Paradise

start
here

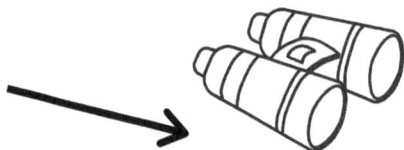

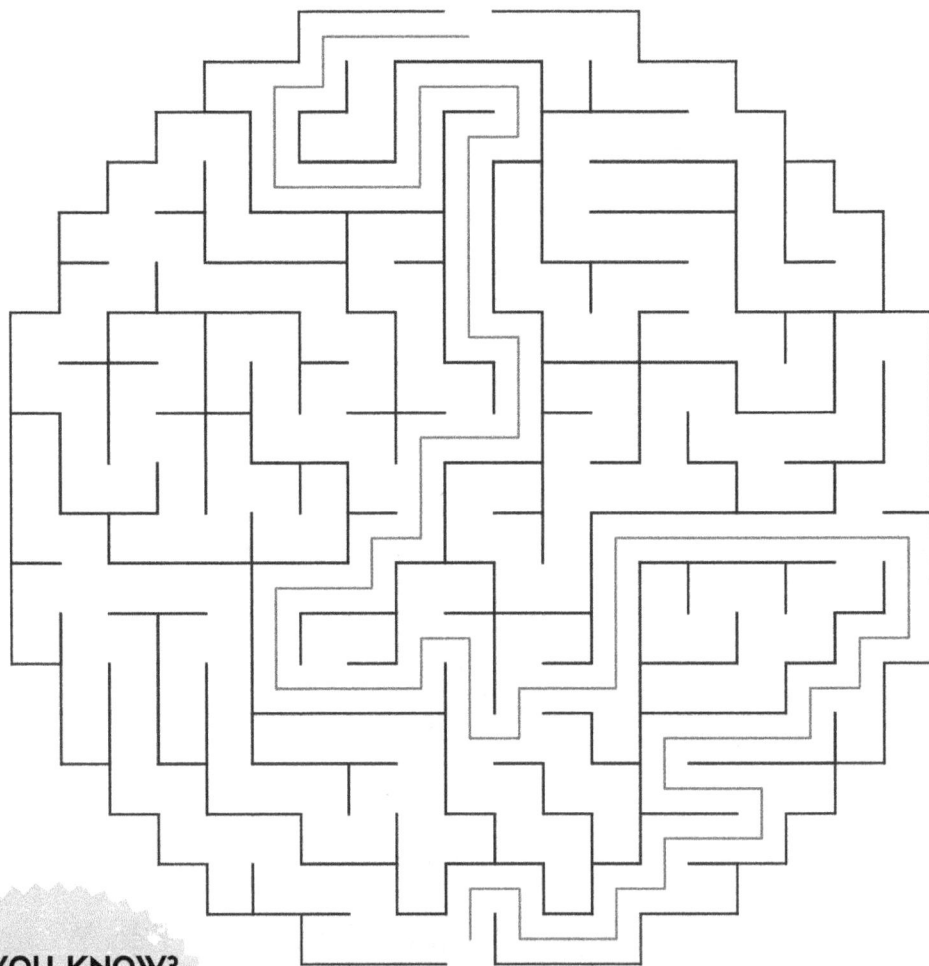

DID YOU KNOW?
Mount Rainier is home to several birds of prey, including eagles, hawks, and owls. Birds of prey are birds that hunt other animals for food.

Answers: Who Lives Here?

Below are 12 plants and animals that live in the park.
Use the word bank to fill in the clues below.

word bank: pika, huckleberry, grand fir, elk, mink, mountain lion, beaver, coyote, tiger lily, bobcat, porcupine, paintbrush

MINK
BOBCAT
HUCKLEBERRY
MOUNTAIN LION
COYOTE
PORCUPINE
PAINTBRUSH
PIKA
GRAND FIR
TIGER LILY
ELK
BEAVER

Find the Match!
Common Names and Latin Names

Match the common name to the scientific name for each animal. The first one is done for you. Use clues on the page before and after this one to complete the matches.

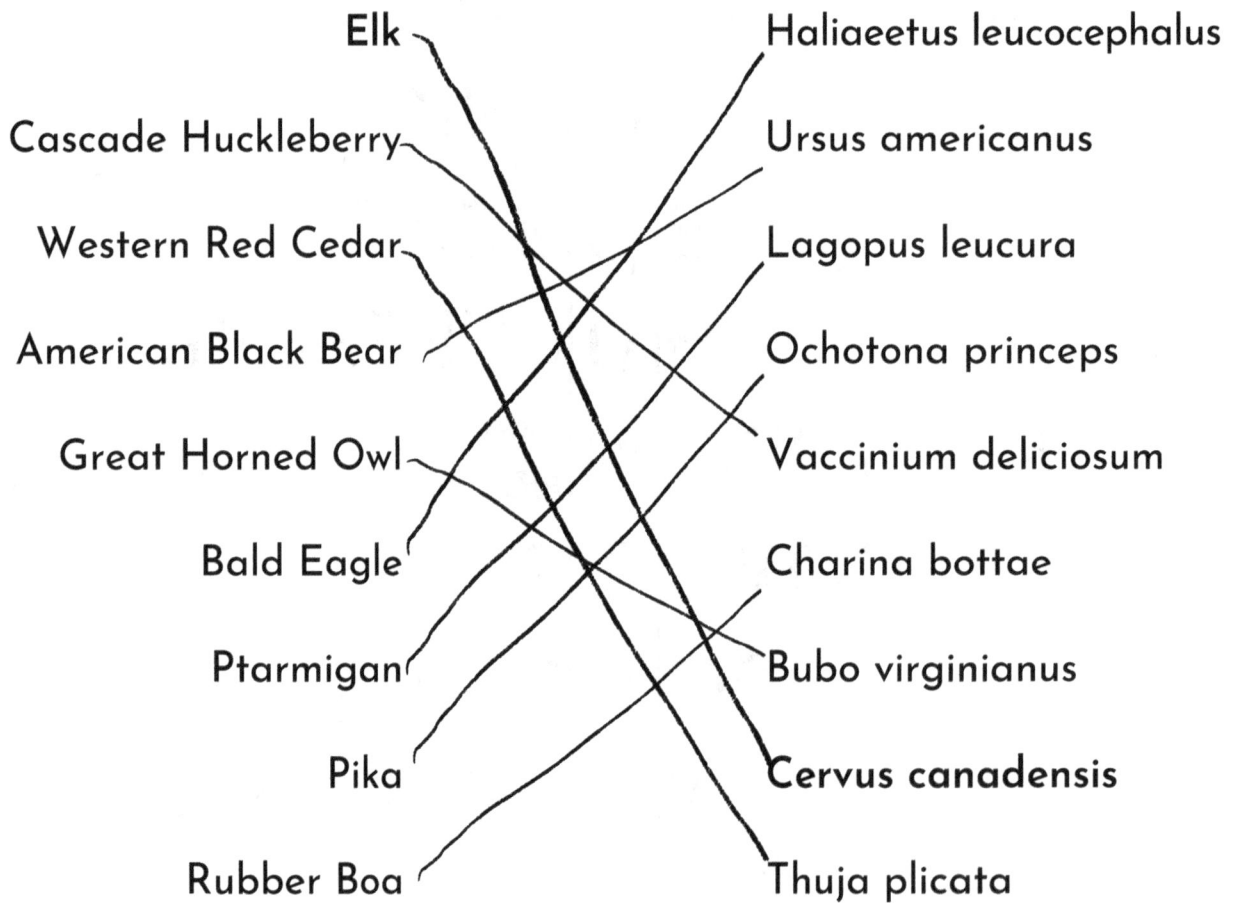

Elk   Haliaeetus leucocephalus

Cascade Huckleberry   Ursus americanus

Western Red Cedar   Lagopus leucura

American Black Bear   Ochotona princeps

Great Horned Owl   Vaccinium deliciosum

Bald Eagle   Charina bottae

Ptarmigan   Bubo virginianus

Pika   Cervus canadensis

Rubber Boa   Thuja plicata

Bald Eagle

Haliaeetus leucocephalus

Answers: The Ten Essentials

Careful preparation and knowledge are key to a successful adventure into Mount Rainier National Park's backcountry.

The ten essentials are a list of things that are important to have when you go for longer hikes. If you go on a hike to the <u>backcountry</u>, it is especially important that you have everything you need in case of an emergency. If you get lost or something unforeseen happens, it is good to be prepared to survive until help finds you.

The ten essentials list was developed in the 1930s by an outdoors group called the Mountaineers. Over time and technological advancements, this list has evolved. Can you identify all the things on the current list? Circle each of the "essentials" and cross out everything that doesn't make the cut.

(fire: matches, lighter, tinder, and/or stove)	~~a pint of milk~~	~~extra money~~	(headlamp, plus extra batteries)	(extra clothes)
(extra water)	~~a dog~~	~~Polaroid camera~~	~~bug net~~	~~lightweight game like a deck of cards~~
(extra food)	~~a roll of duct tape~~	(shelter)	(sun protection, such as sunglasses, sun-protective clothes and sunscreen)	(knife, plus a gear repair kit)
~~a mirror~~	(navigation: map, compass, altimeter, GPS device, or satellite messenger)	(first aid kit)	~~extra flip-flops~~	~~entertainment like video games or books~~

Backcountry - a remote undeveloped rural area.

Mount Rainier Word Search

Words may be horizontal, vertical, diagonal, or they might be backwards!

1. glacier
2. ridge
3. peak
4. volcano
5. lakes
6. Cascade
7. entrance
8. Tahoma
9. wildflowers
10. climbers
11. Paradise
12. Longmire
13. snowshoe
14. salmon
15. marmots
16. ferns
17. Aurora Lake
18. Nisqually
19. Puyallup
20. meadow

```
C W I L D F L O W E R S A O K
H T P E A K O E S H E R N R J
T E P O K A N O C C L A A P B
S M P H S P G U C A C L U M C
P E A S A L M O N L I U J K L
U O L W Y W I O O A T E A C I
Y E A O A R R V C P B R I A M
A C C N M L E N T A H O M A B
L N H S E E L O E E S D S P E
L A I C A B O Y G L A C I E R
U R A H D C M C D N M E A C S
P T N I O M O A I M O K I D I
I N O S W O I S R J R A Q N E
O E G T L E V E S M S R V E F
N I S Q U A L L Y E O O H E E
X J T F I R E F K I E T Q N R
U E S I D A R A P E T P S E N
A U R O R A L A K E M A L A S
```

58

Answers: Find the Match!
What are Baby Animals Called?

Match the animal to its baby. The first one is done for you.

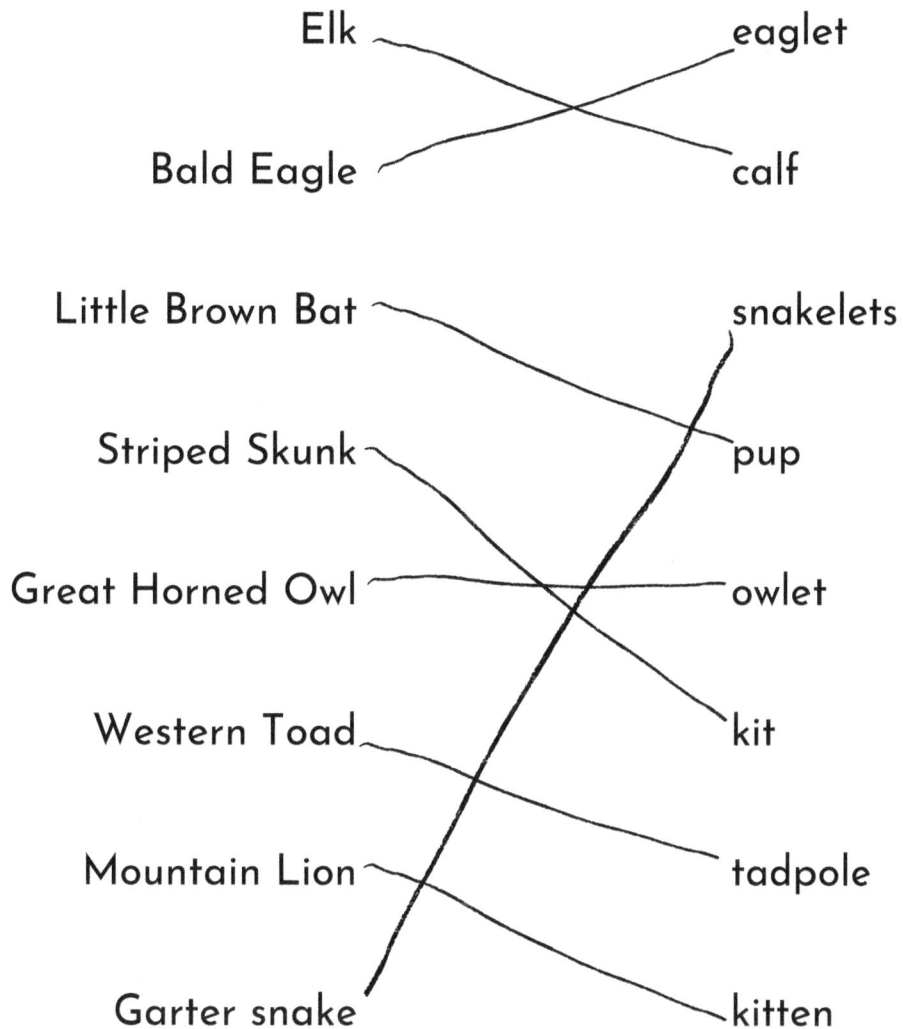

Elk — eaglet

Bald Eagle — calf

Little Brown Bat — snakelets

Striped Skunk — pup

Great Horned Owl — owlet

Western Toad — kit

Mountain Lion — tadpole

Garter snake — kitten

Wildlife Wisdom

The national park is home to a lot of different kinds of animals. Seeing wildlife can be an exciting thing about visiting the national park but it is important to remember that these animals are wild. They need plenty of space and a healthy habitat where they can find their own food. Part of this is not allowing animals to eat any human food. This is their home and we are the visitors. We need to be respectful of the wildlife in the park.

Directions: Circle the highlighted words that best complete the following sentences.

If an animal changes its behavior because of your presence, you are:
    A) too close
    B) funny looking
    C) dehydrated and should drink more water

The best thing we can do to help wild animals survive is:
    A) make them pets
    B) protect their habitat
    C) knit them winter sweaters

In a national park, it is okay to share your food with wild animals:
    A) never
    B) always
    C) sometimes

When you're hiking in an area where there are bears, you should warn bears that you are entering their space by:
    A) hiking quietly
    B) making noise
    C) wearing bright colors

At night, park rangers care for the animals by:
    A) putting them back into their cages
    B) tucking them into bed
    C) leaving them alone

If you see an abandoned bird's nest, it is best to:
    A) pet the baby birds
    B) leave it alone
    C) crunch the empty eggshells

Bears look under logs in hopes of finding:
    A) granola bars
    B) insects
    C) peanuts to eat

The place where an animal lives is called its
    A) condo
    B) habitat
    C) crib

Solution: Hike to a Glacier

Glaciers of Mount Rainier
Word Search

1. Carbon
2. Cowlitz
3. Edmunds
4. Emmons
5. Flett
6. Inter
7. Kautz
8. Nisqually
9. Ohanapecosh
10. Paradise
11. Puyallup
12. Pyramid
13. Russell
14. Sarvant
15. Success
16. Whitman
17. Wilson
18. Winthrop

```
C W E M M O N S E S K L O W K
H O D T M I L Z S H E R W R N
T H M R K I N T E R P B A O B
S A U A S P R U C E U L B M S
C N N I S Q U A L L Y R J K U
A A D D Y W O K D B A E A C C
R P S D P R E G A C L R I A C
P E B A M E I N W I L S O N E
R C H P G E L O B E U D S P S
E O I R Y B O Y H I P G O T S
Q S A U A R I C N N E E N C N
S H N S K W A I S M S K I R E
I J O S F H I M Z T I L W O C
J Y G E L I V E I O D R V E O
N W X L K T A B E D A O H E M
T T E L F M E G S A R V A N T
U A E E S A E N N E A P V E B
C J D W I N T H R O P A L A S
```

Answers: Leave No Trace Quiz

1. How can you plan ahead and prepare to ensure you have the best experience you can in the National Park?

     A. Make sure you stop by the ranger station for a map and to ask about current conditions.

2. What is an example of traveling on a durable surface?

     A. Walking only on the designated path.

3. Why should you dispose of waste properly?

     C. So that other peoples' experiences of the park are not impacted by you leaving your waste behind.

4. How can you best follow the concept "leave what you find?"

     B. Take pictures but leave any physical items where they are.

5. What is not a good example of minimizing campfire impacts?

     C. Building a new campfire ring in a location that has a better view.

6. What is a poor example of respecting wildlife?

     A. Building squirrel houses out of rocks from the river so the squirrels have a place to live.

7. How can you show consideration of other visitors?

     B. Wear headphones on the trail if you choose to listen to music.

All in the Day of a Park Ranger

There are many right answers for this activity, but not all of the provided examples are good activities for a park ranger. In fact, a park ranger's job may include stopping visitors from doing some of these things.

The list below has activities that rangers do not do:

feed the migratory birds

throw rocks off the side of the mountain

pick wildflowers

share marshmallows with squirrels

catch frogs or toads and make them race

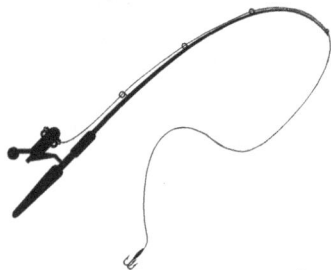

Solution: Catch a Fish in the Nisqually River

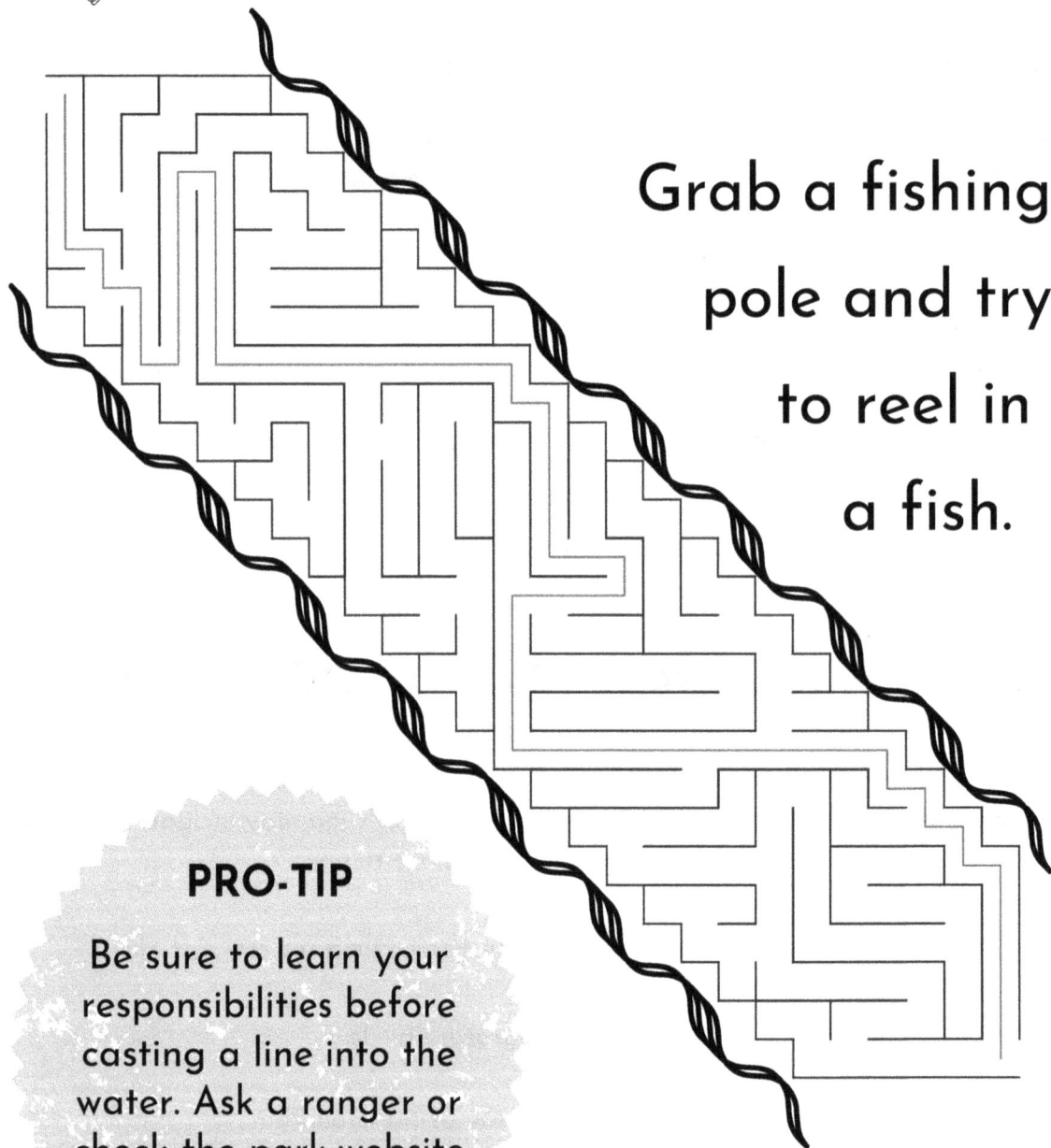

Grab a fishing pole and try to reel in a fish.

PRO-TIP

Be sure to learn your responsibilities before casting a line into the water. Ask a ranger or check the park website before you go.

Crack the Code

Use the code to figure out some fun facts about Mount Rainier National Park

ANSWER: A B C D E F G H I J K L M N O P Q R S T U V W Y
CODE: O T D A J K E F Y L R Q S W I G N H P U V M C B

What is the most visited glacier in the park?

N I S Q U A L L Y
W Y P N V O Q Q B

Mount Rainier is the tallest mountain in this mountain range.

C A S C A D E
D O P D O A J

Seismological research happens at Mount Rainier. What is seismology the study of?

E A R T H Q U A K E S
J O H U F N V O R J P

The Land of the Puyallup

There are six tribes that have connections to the lands and resources found within the current boundaries of Mount Rainier National Park. The Puyallup Tribe is just one of those groups. The Tribe has a reservation to the northeast of the mountain. Complete the crossword puzzle below to learn more about the Puyallup people.

Word Bank

TAHOMA
URBAN
CULTURE
WASHINGTON
MEDICINE CREEK
FISHING
BERRY-PICKING
LUSHOOTSEED
ART
POTLATCH
CEDAR

Across and Down grid:

3. POTLATCH
5. FISHING
6. BERRYPICKING
8. LUSHOOTSEED
10. URBAN
11. ART

1. MEDICINE CREEK
2. WASHINGTON
4. CULTURE
7. CEDAR
9. TAHOMA

Down

1. The treaty that the US government created to take land away from the Puyallup and neighboring tribes.

2. Modern-day state where many Puyallup People live.

4. This is ever-evolving and includes the customs, arts, social institutions, and achievements of a people group.

7. A type of tree important to Puyallup life used to make clothing, homes, and canoes.

9. A Puyallup name for Mount Rainier.

Across

3. A traditional event that centers around gift-giving, food, song, storytelling, and gathering

5. An important traditional and cultural activity related to food.

6. Gathering of blackberries, salmonberries, and other berries

8. The Puyallup people traditionally spoke a dialect of this language. Many speak it today.

10. The Puyallup reservation is this, meaning much of their land is within a city-like environment.

11. Creative activities that express imaginative or technical skill. It produces a product, an object.

Solution: Go Snowshoeing at Longmire

Help find Parker's winter hat!

start here →

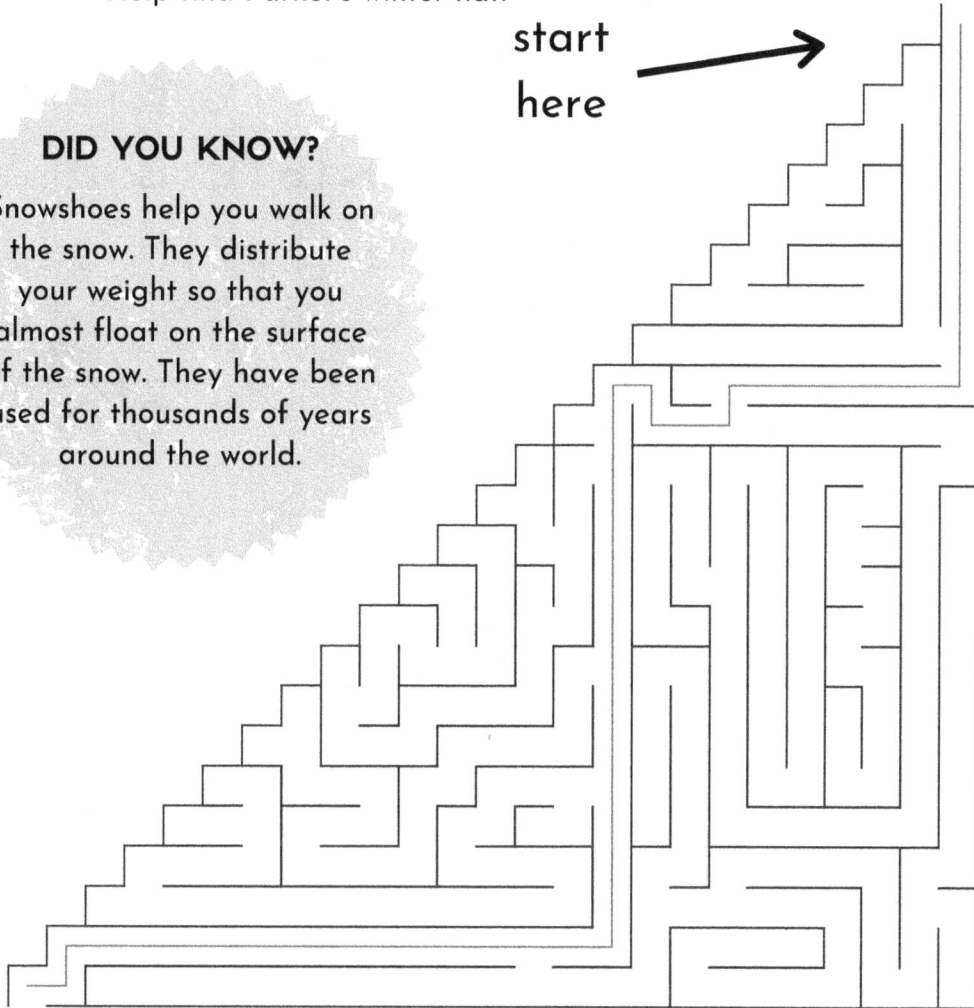

Let's Go Camping
Word Search

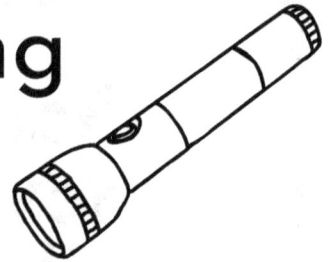

1. tent
2. camp stove
3. sleeping bag
4. bug spray
5. sunscreen
6. map
7. flashlight
8. pillow
9. lantern
10. ice
11. snacks
12. smores
13. water
14. first aid kit
15. chair
16. cards
17. books
18. games
19. trail
20. hat

```
D P P I L L O W D B T E A C I
E O A D P R E A A M B R C A N
P W C A M P S T O V E I H X G
R A H S G E L E B E E D A P S
E L B U G S P R A Y N G I E A
S I A H G C I C N N M E R C N
C W N L A F I R S K O O B F K
M T A E M I L E L H M R W L J
T A P R E A O R E S L B A A B
S M P A S R R T E N T L U S C
C E A I I R C G P E I U J H A
S S N A C K S S I M O K I L R
I J R S F O I S N J R A Q I D
C Y E T L E V E G U O R V G S
E W T A K C A B B S S O H H M
X J N F I R S T A I D K I T T
U A A E S S E N G E T P V A B
C J L I A R T D N A M A H A S
```

68

Fish at Mount Rainier

1.

2.

3.

Unscramble the common names of these fish that live in the park.

4.

5.

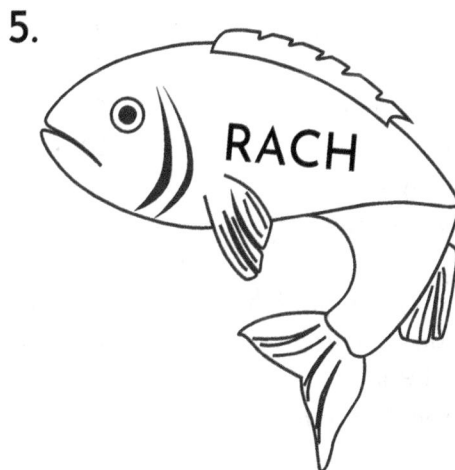

1. __WHITEFISH__
2. __TROUT__
3. __SALMON__
4. __SCULPIN__
5. __CHAR__

Word Bank

salmon
sunfish
trout
minnow
sculpin
char
whitefish
catfish

Answers: Other National Parks Crossword

Besides Mount Rainier National Park, there are 62 other diverse and beautiful national parks across the United States. Try your hand at this crossword.

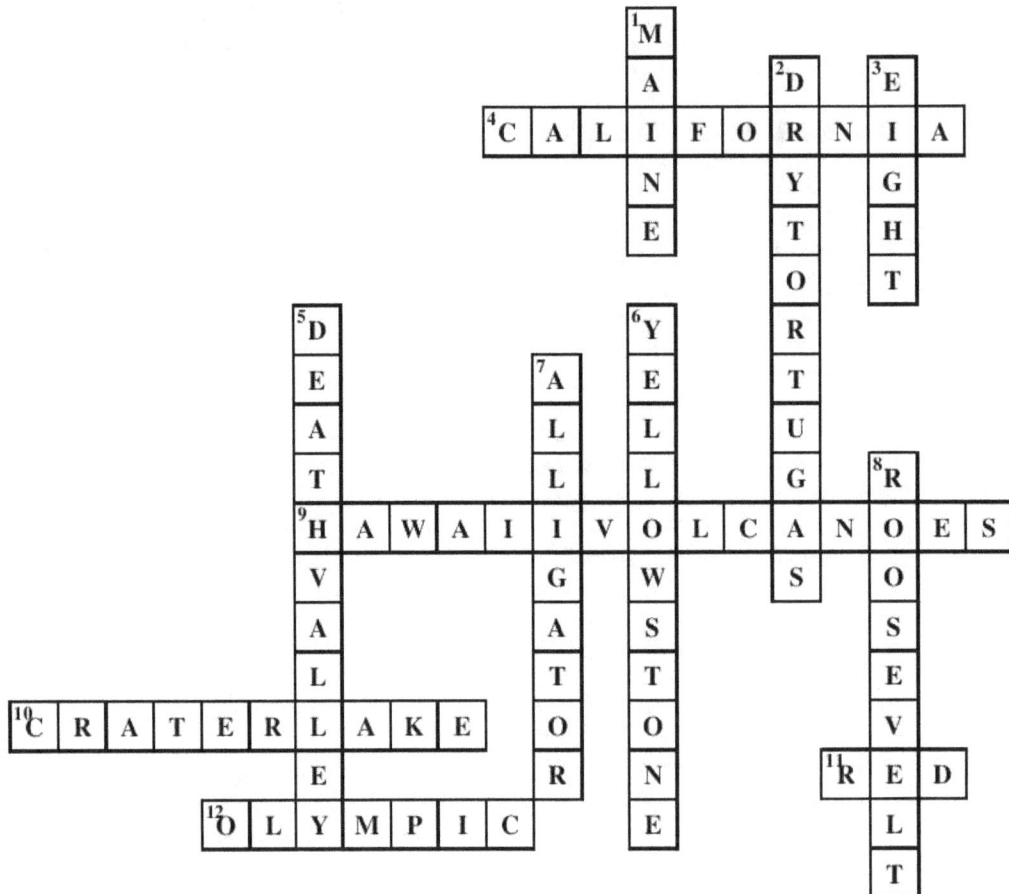

Crossword solution grid:

- 1 Down: MAINE
- 4 Across: CALIFORNIA
- 2 Down: DRYTORTUGAS
- 3 Down: EIGHT
- 5 Down: DEATHVALLEY
- 6 Down: YELLOWSTONE
- 7 Down: ALLIGATOR
- 8 Down: ROOSEVELT
- 9 Across: HAWAIIVOLCANOES
- 10 Across: CRATERLAKE
- 11 Across: RED
- 12 Across: OLYMPIC

Down

1. State where Acadia National Park is located
2. This National Park has the Spanish word for turtle in it
3. Number of National Parks in Alaska
5. This National Park has some of the hottest temperatures in the world
6. This National Park is the only one in Idaho
7. This toothsome creature can famously be found in Everglades National Park
8. Only president with a national park named for them

Across

4. This state has the most National Parks
9. This park has some of the newest land in the US, caused by a volcanic eruption
10. This park has the deepest lake in the United States
11. This color shows up in the name of a National Park in California
12. This National Park deserves a gold medal

Answers: Which National Park Will You Go To Next?

1. Zion
2. Big Bend
3. Glacier
4. Olympic
5. Sequoia
6. Bryce
7. Mesa Verde
8. Biscayne
9. Wind Cave
10. Great Basin
11. Katmai
12. Yellowstone
13. Voyageurs
14. Arches
15. Badlands
16. Denali
17. Glacier Bay
18. Hot Springs

```
F M M E S A V E R D E B N E Y
E A B I G B E N D E S A S E M
Y L I C A L O Y N E E D L T G
D M G A S S A U C N R L U E R
C E L I I T S C R E O A A K E
S N A W Y E E O I W T N A C A
G I C H A A Q C S E M D N S T
N O I Z P R U T I M R S N E B
I W E L M P O N B W E B K H A
R J R F D N I F L I H B U C S
P A B E E S A N E S O P W R I
S J A E N Y A C S I B A U A N
T C Y I A D O H H Y M E A L R
O T A T L M L E S E G R W R J
H S T O I K A T M A I R O P B
I C H U R C O L Y M P I C O U
O Y G T S D E O S B R Y C E T
W I N D C A V E I N R O H E M
```

www.ingramcontent.com/pod-product-compliance
Lightning Source LLC
Chambersburg PA
CBHW080426030426
42335CB00020B/2612